Anne Portugal

absolute bob

translated from the French
by Jennifer Moxley

Burning Deck / Anyart, Providence

SERIE d'ECRITURE is an annual of current French writing in English translation. The first five issues were published by SPECTACULAR DISEASES, which continues to be a source for European distribution and subscription. Since No. 6, the publisher has been Burning Deck in Providence, RI.
Editor: Rosmarie Waldrop

Individual copies $14. Subscription: 2 issues $24.
Supplements: $8, gratis to subscribers.

Distributors:
Small Press Distribution, 1341 Seventh St,. Berkeley CA 94710
1-800/869-7553; www.spdbooks.org
www.audiatur.no/bokhandel
Spectacular Diseases, c/o Paul Green, 83b London Rd., Peterborough, Cambs. PE2 9BS
US subscriptions: Burning Deck, 71 Elmgrove Ave., Providence RI 02906
krwaldrop@earthlink.net

Burning Deck Press is the Literature Program of ANYART: CONTEMPORARY ARTS CENTER, a tax-exempt (501c3), non-profit organization.

The cover photograph is by Kristin P. Bradshaw.

ISSN 0269-0179
ISBN9 78-1-936194-02-5
Originally published as *définitif bob*
© 2002 P.O.L. Editeur
Translation © 2010 by Jennifer Moxley

SERIE d'ECRITURE
No. 23

absolute bob

1

Now that he has popped
up on the earth
cause til now he's
the last one to watch

and dig nothing but
sky found below and
inside the column
the lift off
of working this way
to have them at hand
the house floorplan
which you'd better be aware of

that's the thing he wanted and to get it
he clamped on his iron pillows
to hear the tv he's inside of
but backwards and inside out

his swell living room a perfect antique
joined to whoever is
his double and digs him
for having got off the ground

and that's how bob can
push open a door
a simple door not
a door like that
but nonetheless
automatically opened
door and door
free on the floor
he is really a demon
with a determined voice
you think me an oldster
but I am not
accident aftermath
the vitality of white snow
we become investors

the cellphone he'll find
a reason
for the one who
has given him
this copper button

he says okay let's start

blue spring hinge
bleu fleur
in the woods bob has found
an intense horizontal mission
an address that includes adam's name
right next to the other one
animal life or some such thing

bob says to himself run he runs he runs he dies
the noise of a tiny butterfly
indicator of the touch fluorescent

and here he is crossing the forest that looks like the path through
    a park
an hour at most until he arrives by avoiding
the place the fields here's the green
disrupted path

he can take to avoid
the fork ahead
only I must
he suddenly thought
not these woods again
I must get back to the house

the other way often he loses
and when he loses it's two times too-wide turns
even these beautiful sights the beautiful church
eight days to really see

and the path now
twelve ravines
to get to a good friend

to move through the door with each try
an increasingly feeble grip

if he wants to move his heart forward
to cure love's declaration
and instructions
"no matter how red
as for my heart I will hold on to it
tomorrow if I want to move forward
it is a matter of worry o destiny"
a path in the woods
the counterfeit attraction of a green outfit

intense action jingle bell to better see the place say o or think of death
logical hare appearing

2

Endless the entryway stay without end
at creation's beginning but afterwards

the indicators of tendencies
first
second
third act of his body like he said
with the existing material

and that's how bob can place the vibration label
with a longer muzzle
intact green shocks of the outside watch out for the ether
low reactor carved in wood

drawing paper seeded with stars the wise-ass again
who eats him like food
and champagne
this way allowing the sweetness
to lift off the wish to touch down
couldst thou be the girl isolde recoiling
flashing thy break lights
but afterward escaping gulping down the pro-
visions a girl aloft her weight on board
siphon the eiderdown arrange the picture and look through
the shutter to see what's up with the weather

seen quickly advancing
seen swooping below
running
he sees
hefty cargo
maximum drift

pure blood lamb
no flame no telephone
the eek noise is enough
a shiver in his building
and for more security
wrapped in many
packages chasing all
rubber eek
camera vibrations

grants all along
got on the wall giants
built communally the area
easy to locate
the combo-universe
baby seems cold to him
redrawing his clouds
has just given up
cargo upset

and that's how bob can by breaking down doors
exaggerate shrimp the living room color
his relationship a medium-warm fur coat
as he comes within view of animals
forcing the naming of clara the islands clara showing the way
to be a smooth proton ornament
this enormous portal how having created it
he was partial to it and copied it
and so it is and
does nothing but maneuver
inside its frame

place dismantled do you want it
salmon private lakeside boxwood
paved hardware vevey
just getting to the crowd effect
the line ends at the key of c

3

Confidential groupings conscious organs
super ugly gear
from a history with an irresistible future
nevertheless time presses on he has only

a low table on a base of hospitality
next comes hope
the curve of a culture of voyages
physical need
a skewed photo of nothing but a classified place

remained fixed
to the cliff

but that's how bob can better defend the objects in the background
the meaning of the word lightbulb the darkness
is the subject dealt with squared
really the silent one the great one
seen without stopping end-to-end volcano
moves forward by fire alone-o

the fire two words traction i.e. sport
splits the soul by going homophonic
the future with and on them for a moment
classical roots the regrets
the large round frame will work better

on the other hand it is better than an impression
of other skies a plan to see them again soon
to speak louder a shifting like that of
glass greenery where we pass into form
rather than play the delicate one

that's how he can enunciate the rule of decision
at his request each time more exhausting more cabaret-like
the container that sways
the sand bag that sways
balks at appearing
ambassador

flees by train in the guise of a stockbroker
and his control
gone down a level
footstool
elephant drive in the countryside

the image of the donor at the roundabout
at the moment of rushing
off to the zoo
makes the introductions moves timidly forward
busy with flagstones while speaking of tombs
moves back
a correspondent whom memory keeps equally present

bob slides himself to
the spot where
narcotic effects
the language of paradise touches everything
gets near
noticed by the insects
he pushed the world
wrapped tabula table set
soft talc facing the wood's undergrowth the wood settles

and that's how bob can act excellently when withdrawing
the particular dwarf that slapped him
by naming becomes his own dwarf the one who gave him
his random form of sleep does not exist

really put on the spot
participated did all that and
thanks to the mirror
touched the reversible whaa whaa region

4

That same day the first sounds were english
someone who smoked cigarettes always on tv
partition slashed sofa backrest
plastic object filmed object

surface decorations
and more ideas
the thing is he's busy
at least alone
a room with a mirror
a bed right next to him
long or at least
recuperative

and that's how bob can eliminate the connections with an independent
    cable

the likely friends distance the converging lines
the floor at mid-path as soon as the true blue sky arrives
automobile also some dust

arrow at the back of the living room
the sunken hall a step down he chose it what gaze
comes back to him from the right-facing window
his step is also the answer
in other words a straight shot at the earth

eyes follow the reel
moist but not from the smoke
white utilized this principle
of the guides of explorers
detaching them from the background

corridor the so-called life of someone
the trajectory of sand down the docks
produces a very beautiful shadow
before the see-through screens
a crack that sets free ants

he sees the sources determined
black shadows translated
nor are there faces inside there until
going out again into the world
there is an electrician standing up straight

he can jump over a square
beef up his breathing
maybe imagine
an athletic event
with golden handlebars

in case of serious equality
storm the overhang
the max perhaps
classify flora and fauna
by their wintry beauty

each type of conduct available by catalog
at ease his reserves evoke a passage
the outside defined like the space
surrounding a free afternoon
is the opposite of his prison
touching the wall to be noticed
the light emanating from the ceiling
linear and so extending the halo
that clothes the scene
limit of a universal split
an enterprise without guaranty

he will be the victor who
can line up
a marvelous bird
if he has none
he will give none

5

To get a foot in the living room
simple drawing reproduction
with deceptive dimensions

there he has is only the the lower lip
of two kneeling shepherds
perfectly extremely equal in length
an ass a lamb

the duplicates of each plan
in the service of suits
moved back to a different date

bird is the only true copy
so quickly the only way

and that's how bob with his scythe can introduce himself
as able to subtly blend in with the place
to see in the town as well
flowering green flowerbeds
the double annunciation
with an air so
red wine white

accompanying signs
sport "equipment for"
france "the garden of"
a building "a wing of the same"
like on the day of its construction

is also a place of youth
height of the door
unique condition
the gallery-prototype
the noise of his step
a decoy
through the smoke-screen

and that's how bob can use the unoccupied villager role
order the vulture reproduce the irritators on the skin
the balls
the blindness of a specialist
with a typical office
construct observation towers that extend
the origins of humanity

the idea in the option and how he climbs up there before using the
instruments the exteriors a pancreas of normal size
ready to accept it without any conditions
not altered
he regenerates
through the backdoor
the slightest gesture in the face of chance

so much more the expert
all alone
not a single open passage
the bench being pleather there is a difference
morning strip of sky
midday tv picture

and that's how bob can infiltrate the grid mid-groove
the intervals not a charm he considers them
of countrified taste haphazard reference
and of the mix of scenery which surrounds
he dusts his feet off lights a fire transports the relics
until o wonder the panel moves and continues masculine
the archers the archers the archers the archers the archers
invisible mock up the chinese woman near the storage wells

his direction set towards her or the sky
but he can't see on the negative's surface
any object insisting he love in the future
not even in the background
wall yellow wall with the clause à tuer to kill
begins at a dance he wants to drive this voice
bodily cascade trajectory followed by a bridge
two glassed-in bay windows in the local style

refining the attempts
where the results would be the remainder
a war set-up the upset
understands how he wanted just to know
if on a given subject the idea of doing it
outdated permission luck at last
and followed it with a number of complaints
and demands

6

Stalling blocking creature
chinese motor that makes all cats grey
must plug in and expand
the place that is his
so it changes
right there so it changes the triggered effects
reconnect around the ear with nothing a ribbon
outline the hand
the air leaves
raised a wire
signal

but by and large there is consensus

and that's how bob can localize on the surface the supported instants
columns
block wire capacity
at his command
seventy-eight brains plugged-in reverse speed
explore in bulk
shift fruits and grains by fits and starts
they want to change that and this hope
with the aid of the inside operator
goes further into the picture than into
the beautiful object the outcome
wears a helmet
serenity
happy state when watertightness is the sign of a beautiful summer

on the outline of a circle
photo
painted town
connection small arc
of a dive outlined from there
classic canal pontoon

in this order the canvas the refuge
distemper on wood
and in his mouth a swallowing action
grey and on the inside
the cash resister against the wall loose paving stones

and that's how bob already so familiar can make free time for himself
a panel slides garden
still a living one who speaks
road without more waiting
noble white air and the name of every songbird
created family plantations rooms to sleep in
the current suddenly counts on sparking

seen naked arms
black lacquer cabinet silver hair
all these treasures are his

there are shoulders as well as arms
crossed
resting on him resting out of view

and that's how bob can after option
bounce back better on his armor
stretches shudders shines the standards
of islands appropriate to his open
heart and said
to give also
to spend for things
to stop why that's impressive
a clarity about couches
tasting the twilght
putting up pink bills
moving one armchair then another
suddenly leaden

the veranda becomes the main street again

7

Considering titles gripping the floor
of the next anchor store that offered a view of the whole
he has only four quarters of the property
the only shadow in range a section
segmented of the cross of saint-flour
a month that has only 28 days
sun and moon at the same time

most of the stuff's bought up
triggering the next step
emptiness in its place
because of the dates makes him spontaneously suspend filtration
for and between the clouds

but that's how bob can admirably fake it in order to get bold colors
there's not one pic not true
in cabaret and style a spectral marrow
wood crescents crash down again
at his feet violets blue rug
unless it is just air

the whole thing in poly-vision
in the pure danger sky
deadly cry that he was a nice guy

maybe not hurried for nothing
even if he turns subject
the telltale corner of a street
blocked by a black car
model of this gem the everyday

murder in the business
district in the end casts him
touches-up that he was a nice guy

so no opportunity and nothing seen
a share of the outcome
the cut
could well light up the individual
the heart's dark green obsession

and speaking of tearing up logic
you can tell by the way he walks
his only regret is that he was a nice guy

no way there's no laugh
intentions he returns them
accidents cold yellows gold
pelluqueria by other means
the excessive blond of death

makes the mirror idea stick
so that it seems the holy face
admitted he was a nice guy

without interest because no one
told him to cut the pine branch
blood-spitting image where by
at the height of age rust at last
intersecting two hares

each distinguishing itself
the joining of one end
to the other that he was a nice guy

doesn't make it no really there's no more
indigo placebo on the right side
delicate and diverse bits
blues to mix
the examples do not link up

selector torches
in secret girl talk
that he was a nice guy

not of himself nor a sign
but an impulse he suspects
that she was a babe and took her compact
a brain of a lover a body modelled
on the movies really

and the immobility of pink neon
and for that same reason
admit that he was a nice guy

no time his effort to take nothing
removing him is a military feat
he looks tired his hair
sparse his fear is it
bangs of fire time's needle in the red

of its chance exhibition
where he breathes more easily savors
the argument that he was a nice guy

no desire to share nothing
approaches the sound track still asleep
obvious plots of all night movies
the point of saying has passed
I'm going back a ways

unfasten its equipment
reduce the disc circuit
the repetitive he was a nice guy

8

Contract
cell thought to be next in line he has
in the records of cornice reconnoitering
only the parade's final part
two feet to end it
the length arranging with full support
the stomach recumbent evoking
a very oblique strain of sympathy

see the following foreshortened
the first sign of the eye
the hare as buddy
"let's get out of here"
and that's how bob can refer without transition to this picture of
    efficiency
hare like straw an eye an eye for the twofold field
yellow cut so he espied the slice

for the others he might say
unknown hare branches
then goes on to play comparative plateau
the third with
the fourth with
the mystical at their backs
a sign of spring

and that's how bob can explore the making of lilacs
twice underline his instrumental certainty
his heart on board
his skin on board
the hour arrived
delicate painting of objectivity
the build-up enchants
behind the screen
the edge of the bowl the crackle of pop
corn including dumbbells and bloatings
the strong secret of the air removes
one color after another
and everything happens in black and white
the world and all
and desire and the lamb

the next step
of what works for this that way
the next step
if the space is narrow
if it cracks then falls
five men surrounding matisse-like
by details and events
in short gracious in their verbalizations
things that he names
like some
bitchy blonde called
pegasus
one wall one dot

he has reset the uses of his tv circuit

and that's how bob can bend negatives
creating his very own accident

a single
accident
elsewhere
bridge
tight dress
shattered white
and maybe
something that didn't go

always hurried moved discolored
in short my pet has only
this year's dress
from a bunch of willows
far from the bank
later the sight of her beauty
the iris seen by other plants
vaguely hoped for a little speed
from an arm held above the head
without any reason to be there

9

Order to go back to beauty plane-trees avenue
crystal competition snow and cold
move about tablecloth spread out
the dinner is frozen a passing bear
strong liqueurs horse on a tear
the ball has been started by the herd
crowned dolphin with jellied herbs
a haunch of deer a passing boar
ginger pâté and horse gay
hot pepper wine wolf so fine

but that's how bob can probe the big chill hypothesis
blind so high up has solved the roof shingle shine problem
yes all the same where everything holds the installation
didn't want to divide up normal life
a system for arousing emotion
comes out of the fridge to find himself among the dead
has pulled the three levers and from behind the girl in ambush

a sleeve of air and the cliffs yesterday's reception the breeze
and he is convinced that it's no good
the ceiling light the faults in the mechanism
what he did was no good go and he wants to keep
the water's edge
the course of life altered the chair he rocks
ducking back into the corridor shall be connected to the principal
    corpse landscape

cleaning and one and two hidden portraits
a different voice fragile so that one isn't sure
if a character moves detaches and who becomes
the face deflated
jap jap the switch helps to save it
old age thoughts under construction
he reclassifies the wire in an electronic schism

had a foot in this place
that is to say a second a marvel to take him away
and he lifts up his outfit clears his lungs
unwinds the machine at the apex
the exact idiom of the idea
that a door leads to death via the intermediary of his hand
that he recognizes the smoke-stained apartment plaques

for an admirer the excuse
essentially on each box he must snuff it out
the body is all finished
glass on the ground glass of water detail and a pin
and when he found himself in front he too is there
a part of the whole
object in the foreground

from the desire to place a fly
this type of dresser-architecture in which the public
letterbox drops its letter
the knife
the she-thief needs him and she cheeps sweetie
in the comparable house identified surface
self-stimulating to sleep with

10

And as for certain causes of the present state
value sinking which equals he has
only the sideways use of a man's body given over to science
a "my boyfriend" richard's pet name
which doesn't suit him at all

will he make no effort passing up vomiting
alcohol unit 4 the configurations

sunday afternoon conversation oh nothing oh nothing a little void
at the feet of saint john the soul allows itself the support of hands
his devotion

but that's how bob can officially resist the pressure of linebreaks

precisely nothing left but to take a walk
determining two floodlights
lit in daytime disorder or his consolation
the resemblance idea a sure thing
the motor noise towards his stronger love
even if even if the encumbrance is strong
an adventure an occasion the film with
it's ok

can't have a day like others for him it's all
about reaching this island it's all that remains
found the distance a map of it the painting
that is on the island there is no word more communal
more made up more religious a possibility seen in tandem
for three months he had everything on a little spot of ground
very well he shoots some footage outdoors
it's ok

and for the equivalent abstainer
posthumous dislocation of
the mouth to be painted in early soundfilms
nothing's scrupulous but the ha
of hammock
and that he works to restore

he mixed the backside of the wall of sound
collision inside the frame
explosion came closer
holding
snow which fell out of nothing a curtain to see
length thick ribbon the bay
its platform

because the airplane that starts far
in the cool air remains there

but that's how bob can not see the countryside
and take radar
the king's daughter
he saw he saw he saw
in short he saw excellent reels in independent divisions
opening closing the objects don't move
and finding him totally laugh
nothing to keep him busy
little lizards and no hand

11

At the moment he has only the engraving
the house it does not exist

epilepsy depression a kind of sand
same corridor same room same kitchen
plans that follow
from habit and before which
an accident coming this way

american stylization
there are no closets

always more stretched out when xeroxed
he simultaneously intervenes
rectangular
descriptive
as if a possible
buyer at each place

three adjacent properties
wingtips lightning speed
target state of shock
also a super technical word for saying
hasty hoisting of rocks
today up ahead to crush you
sending of spies and doubtless assassins
target
nothing in particular

he needs
nothing in particular
and he will do
nothing in particular

look here
he sees running
and he sees by the nose
the air
up close to his face
visible
smoke
gesticulation but this shock-absorber
in front is like
a white tuft says
just aim for the head

and that's how bob can
aim at the world and everything
there there on the gate
supporting compartment
when he sees where
painters
at which moment they decide
therefore one of his friends
dies and it's the day
little bears parade
in the courtyard

and that's how bob can try out frenzy for an emotional affect
oh surely he does something curious compromised
includes clothes that are almost alike
hallway sentence and what do you think
finishes the twist

equally in evidence the brick-wall product
moves on to what to expect who'd come in order to
hear him the love of lamentable garlands
it's the right oeuvre on gilded film
the plants in a dark place
though cared for
die a phase of darkness

that she or he the likable one rejects
the first rule is distance
attain the sensational
secondly drunkeness continues
must hold himself up by the arms

serious in the demonstration he adds
a fabrication which interests the moderns
who are a bit mambo
having nothing to pluck the daisy for
nice and woozy
franco-colonial rice factory

slow
ing down choo choo

passionately mam
bo super choo
sawn-off shotgun
and chaos reinforcements

12

Artificial construct outside the studio
that's how he can
stuck there and out-of-sorts
put some nuance in his life

show them while digging out
multiple copies of insistence
stones in the record book
the stated acceptance of double or nothing pick-up sticks

go straight go strong
on top of the mantelpiece
under the doors of walhalla

and everything straightened up might put everything straight
on the equaled surface checked out
put on the bottom shelf what cannot equal
concurrent stability a charmer

his enormous clear
his perch is also the room
where he is busy growing up
he waits and it works

nonchalant sounds
like regulars before
a bell or gong
motives lined up

the table shows the connection of paths
pushes it to maximum
capacity

and that's how bob can sing "plastic pipe" amplified from nothingness
on the air of "oh well these here winds
                    my interior is there
                    my exterior is there"
or of "pegasus can fly but not the winter sky"
pick the pipe back up other rhythms exist
the papa sound the mama sound
just to stick
the vocal imprint that ends in kisses
and for which the theme
being inside speed
must be explained

material on the line

and that's how bob can specify reciprocal grinding
the significance of friction
and move the cursor by two little crosses
this nice o all pink
arrow in the fortification
sounds filtering up a floor
yellow coloring the armoire's bottom drawer
a screen far up in front projecting little crumbs

over his outfit the edge of the sea keeps on
the reaction of multicolored air
produces emotionally moving things
success the world is coming
each day the second wave
the living room is packed

and that's how bob can in testing out the moral law
distance himself more and more bodily
micro-regions inside already
climate saturation renewable by other means
the solid fortification shedding no more pebbles
a large selection of topics he wants to film
a locality a section a square
empty scientifically empty

he sees no fruit in front of him
announcement without a red light
rest of bones that go it alone

pale syrup facing shadow glacial shadow wins

13

To verify in any case that one in front of him leads him
on silent film he only has
thirty-two roses in twenty-six ordinary
vases
navigation
through the growing gap his mouth the noise
does not effect the succession of maps
the insufficiency of truth a local element
a flowering
below still asking for the difference of rich strange

and that's how bob can re-imagine unpublished things
he takes up all the space
on the sidewalk
letting things pass he likes that
seeing things so close up

re-imagine the unpublished things
doctor and throughout it was quite dark
this fatal air if he dared
wait for her below
nervously at each reply
thank you man woman

they didn't see a thing
he leaves indifferent in short he bores
a wasteland but all
included when he got there

re-imagine the unpublished things
and among these cases the expeditious
while on the floor he insists he moves better
with his foot on a stage
the age of the tool is very grueling

re-imagine the unpublished things
a hero why that's a lovely idea
which he also came up with
lightning strikes the ravines beneath his eyes
to die and the film's a stunner

but bob believes everything
there aren't two parts
upper door with exit on it
but seen from high up still up there everywhere the beautiful
horizon bends iron

in the district he saw brigands
all
none
all
none
all
none
excepted
interception a revelation
plus one who talks by himself

but that's how bob can leave a glove behind on a grate
and decide which
working protection stopped
all the wounds inflicted by a blue source
the blocks are going to retaliate

two stakes taken behind
in the night of reinforcements
this order of lightning branches eventually so bent
mummy
museum piece with incredible power
he can transfer it all
man himself and all
four cornered blocks
beyond

green tunnels
parapets above
landscape spillovers
a story like a mining-cart the working of a mine
quick he falls
he can't
jump
he falls from an open convertible

14

The turning walls equivalent sounds
two rows of red searchlights
should confront him bob has only
white skull
the coded version of a flemish air
three intervals
positioned in the background held put
from an echo of his thought
hour nets differently than the light
filtration
of crucial bookmarks
point-by-point topography of the mezzanine
of permanently closed street-facing rooms

but that's how bob can bring about the individual betrayal
his gaze tearful visible enigmatic
                                        nail lance sponge
he orders by express the detailed chaos of the flying dutchman
the bird listening in officially encouraged the inscription
arma christi

randomly goes farther shows his act and disappears
he can add to this these fake clouds
arrangement of figures in the killing field
has changed the crosses
has changed the stones
has changed the benches

a few strides across the lake where his piranha can surface
comes back often
second bureau capharnaum chaos the décor lifts off
in his ear inspired details

in order of distortion
signature in the sludge the physical body the change
slowing down the multiplication he works at
the gaze therefore should come as a reduced wall motif

in night-mode he sleeps in the garden
                                    scissors paper rock
to move back to come closer creates the could-start-crying feeling
the sidelong glance
asking for the insertion of origins for food and gold

finale different hunter gives a feeling of possibility
unidentifiable plants mist on the surface of the lake and the
    evangelical solution
calm down
a cigarette enlivens it will enliven this blend of the photographed
    world

and about a story of chance happenings often lent since
he has only an arranged marriage
the crowning with thorns
bound in a set

put on the surface the i have promised him firmly as he just said
as if in a laboratory one sound has been glued among the high-
    pitched others
elements rigged
c. i. a. his gig

summary of decomposition always to the music
interpreting the role while sitting down and he looks at a view of
    bellevue

but that's how bob can have a conversion and recognize
calendar calendar cancellation something on the inside
excerpt map

in a neon palm tree the voice of objectivity applies
to all things the flower notion
the cause also
sets fake sentences in motion
stem sized the pipe bristles and its function
is something like a new sound
ursa minor mini little cart
miror urbi the mirror
because of interference
one of the two calves sings in latin
the other flies as an example and without moving
still finds bits of heaven

real life no jackpot

it was the picture of correlations
it was the name of the ob-looker

15

Ride in a taxi the sky changes
in brief it is all changed
the sky
and its pearl and its flower
the world in its dress circle
it comes it renews itself the sun gets up
a windmill with blades it's no big deal
in this position
which he represents
he moves and he stretches
tie tips

end transmission

it's a place on the water and for the pylon
all the elements to calmly start the process of being closed up
a classical study the flow of a ditch
and that's how bob can nervous floating
hold back the emission spectrum

made a note at this place
for by repeating "lake" here
where he just passed by took care
noted repeated read just about
finding himself changed

and by a stream each time he sang it was terrific

"lakes lakes I should have come
I saw beneath lakes lakes
I found myself changed
I discovered how one sees
beneath woods above
I saw them lakes lakes
I found myself changed"

clinical secret
the immersions

replays everyone's official forms
humanized made of ice
on the edge of the decoration
and that's how bob can old guy restrictively programmed replay
    the immersions

those that disappear in cold water
food models for the sky
and particularly delightful
gather up in two days
value generally smooth
white bear ophelia

leave combat
torches not without
secret and by a branch
go beyond and then
the rest he knows well
love in cutesy braids

suspicion and more
he sees the top
turn gold his body
he cootchie-cootchie-coos
he sees bad times

in the sense of nuh-uh

and then finding
        t in soft robin
in this way raising arbors
and not able to i dunno
flying spiral strangely
        soft
robin f under which moves
therefore underneath her is
drowned what enchanted so much
        in
soft o robin route of pschitt
the moon goes coldly over
ice cubes and dear great one and
        s

in soft robin is
not revised nor
in any way folded

really good at this side-to-side treatment and from the ground
him whistling only
at juliette's balcony
a potential role and no guests

he has only a scrap of fabric distancing
the heat of his body
these sentence fragments
oh it's you his saliva
a blood of ink i sought you out

and at the hemline less sunlight

16

Seated as he is on the sensible apartment set
singular fire ideal camp
his wishes scattered
in civvies
because he retexturizes the precision of reverberating sound
carefully the nerves the veins
he found striking in the countryside
only the feet properly
and the left arm
amputated
the likelihood that the reference
exercise venue
of the regroupings would not oppose would obey

also the ordinary everywhere
sand and matches
more precisely the india arrangement means just the opposite
a few words in this case i cannot
will serve as alibi

separated and yet still the suitor he loves he longs to love
in accordance with original occidental syntax
so the apparition arrives connected
arrives among the panes of glass

and that's how bob can follow on a diagram
the mood of a nice day beneath the heavens
in freezing a flying fish marvel
the ratio of traits which are no longer
fixed on happiness and now
have you
any news
good reply canal lock pounding
and in the hall there's a glass key that's all
he'll get a topic out of it
he will not look at the final world not at all

and that's how bob can sometimes whistle
"if my desire"
not much more than
"if my desire"

enters the world

like in the void
question both real and fake

no more need
for sideways screens

feeling arms
a mouth offered

central image
of normal cinema

"if my desire
if my desire
the sky is full
if my desire
if my desire really the sky is full"

17

An unforeseen military command to himself
did not exist on paper

in conserving just the opposite
he has not over his shoulder
has not replaced column joint
a sample of urbanism
the level of voices through the keyhole in which rooms
variants near him are painted over his chest
opens up inside collection
pulls at the walls

a fence isolates the trellis
the spacing
will not which is to say might not

his contents on the market
keeps him bound by the shoulders
to the narrow hallway and the small living room

but that's how bob can with regard to metals dislocate from gold bullion
    the orderly investments
he sees the whole mousetrap complicity the moment he makes the change
weight conversion the gutter carried over into the assets
he inserts the aeration duct undresses before going
compressor

state corresponding to privilege
this one an affluence champion coefficient vector
to blast the mountain the points of ennui

size the reverse trans
former not of this world
position of syllables the number which comes up
the equivalent of both
bob and joachim at the golden gate

and that's how bob can make time come back
hermetically beautiful flower
this one frequent
from a bell with a recorded chemical ring
a single schedule bonjour bliss
do it to everyone trace the platinum furrow and make it turn

i stretch my wing
your flower with
the first link to
your thought
has no more basis
key of c drifts se
cret vanity

so that's
what we do to you in your
way in your
tower of thought
fitting words
corpus weighed

sometimes when the supplementary proof
formally forbidden to
flanking
what is a hillock a hill

that's how he can propose delicacies pictures little cuttings
devious or a staged exaltation running his hand through his hair
in the genesis and the moving of movements
bring about a preferable élan removing a sick
constellation

cause of the impression of living showing that he thinks it dead
that all these eventualities that the single source of light
felt in crossing competition the surroundings beginning
a word

asked to introduce like him when laughing things off
his last thank you a line of dialogue of the
continuum type

18

Contemplation over other items
in his basement-located
booth
his head inside
all the changes refused he has
for military action
jumped only to conclusions
the dessert menu
the small dimensions of the topographic
components

sabotage the word
reheat half-acoustic
was used up diminished nonexistent
flowers from the town of nice
chocolate factory

at present he has only his patronymic surname the setting sun
and the evaporation of this heat
heat
a garden apartment on the piazza
horizontal lights
a kind of base
for example oneself
and the rear-view mirror

what he saw
white area
green water literally a flat subject
a sentient basis in an organic world

but that's how bob can stock lifeboat medical kit
sign up for the progressive elaboration
as an amateur volunteer
and profit from the reconstruction

the ascending ramp miraculous profile
recovered by a professional brought back like so
presses his body against understands danced takes refuges on her lap
is beyond franco-swiss jurisdiction
polite
expedites his arms in the night
the breaking news operator returns to
certainty excess baggage
returns to the reports of the even more obvious theological field

if he goes farther he finds
money on the back of fish
before a few ahoys sailing over the oceans

reread dutch translations of paintings
the beautiful park
the reservoirs
the very order of the winds
all full of quicksilver that rises and falls through five-inch pipes
an isolated volume of let's say fifteen pounds
and life-size gutters

a free hand for tristan the prelude
the audience member from the example
in the corridor
and that's how bob can place things in an authentic frame
the craving to say in his own words watch out this is difficult
it is a special kind of work
to identify
the visual
of a doorframe

"do something"
and he sets up the poster
transparently colored

and he paints the pallor of water
for these days of the same color
bronze
enclosed in the universe
usually green breathes in only
green
for all intents and purposes blue
absorbed in the motorcycles the portrait near the others

found his colleague consequently forewarned
and that's how he can control the increase of debits
the critical notations

good-
ie
final phase pigheaded phase
the healing of creatures and their disappearance
enchanted creatures by grace of the grace of the
and the tributes are wooden spheres
flying back together
big chill babies

19

In the narrowness of his ordering
relative
calculated place of a mid-sized interpretation
the abdomen
in the body of saints
overly heavy objects salvaged from an auction sale he has only
one step in twelve
of the back of the dancer who runs from this effect

turning now to the ground he can also
redo the lake bank the other way
with swans coming up really close
the place the idea
of an absolutely identical second chance

luminosity
oh good a reassuring sign
luminosity
the subjective is a combination and that's how bob
can take refuge in a field of clones
a mark on the body
the name is kloop
brilliant rocking
at moments
the telephone's voice
large mouth with string
six tubes recite
kloop kloop
the science of annapurna

each tries one element more
a winch cranking up the narrative
the story he tells ideal
that in this maximum starter we should run
and on this time-tested ground bringing about
any old saga makes a day of life
gallop

that's how he can intentional surface invent the secret
beauty my dear sweet old lady
beauty had been an element of fantasy

theater of operations

spirits in
the white cage in the forest
like finding a needle in a haystack

this chair   very fine
and place it within his range
this cadaver   very fine
and find him a little room to live in
this fairy   very fine
and the affecting poison

fairy not counting unless they're our lot
fairy and yet he thought not
fairy mask of need that's his
fairy there from where she is

affair following demolition
he always bangs up against this kind of stuff

roadmap a schedule

knows it and it is
the same or without
bangings that it isn't
pleasure after
not totally

roadmap a schedule

bonjour heroes
ma'am and if
not too much not so
not able to ob
serve you without you

white finally double which befits
the things that are his glass legs

that's it for the suspicions the dazzling end
of natural history sufficed yes
it has happened yes it is often sufficient
and that's how bob can danger at night
occupy houses
the paintings balancing the woods
he walks through a landscape
outside of
without
then he
the world knows him period

four rivers
lots of snow surrounding
and wall-papering the room
second
adoration of fishes
upright

the body blue the color of hands water green
fingers in the air for example as in "rosette and flowers"
he would like to have himself buried
then cut his throat

but that's how bob can see nothing until at last a presence
should be strong to glaze a giorno his stucco ceiling
around his jaw
the paneled doors close up again
operator in his entirety the corridor delivers him of bee-sieged
    extras
around a black suit
white was asleep
mirror he refused
and likewise two maps of one summer night

impossible we see him use the breaks
alighted hunters shoot on sight

right now he has only a double ax spring
having processed digestive substances worms
sap
all that is inside opposed green
and then keep on going
also passes around the picture
their picture cousins cowboys

in his mouth
breath and breathlessness
hell without recoil
not even red lights

that's how he can terrify the national ocean and it's atmospheric
    admiration
maybe the chain instead of going fetal
where the lights light up
also goes around and it has succeeded
in the south
in the north
with a hook
in the extinction of martian nomenclature

he can test his resistance to promotion
grow pale wink through the window
pane it is closed
and behind there is a garden
blank canvas that by dint
he doesn't even bother to look

so he stays just so he dies if someone
in front of him shows a good face
the spirit of equality he finds reason
happiness for him to have come to grief

                    and in this dream
the lawns were green but how to go about
seeing into their thoughts the street level
many bridges of stone and metal   ₂
sic the second the first the shore there
turning when seen it twists
the view keeps on going
and then an alleyway bob knows nothing about how to live
and so
precipitated movements hello
voila
by heart voila what he's been looking for
the elegance and the comfort of a marvelous bird
and a few coffee dates with the world

21

At the base of the composition two lines of his work
to present it
eliminating it
more easily from breath than eyes he has but one
sparkling chandelier
a night-before baby
changed two times

persuasive reasoning
the slow progressing which leads to the initial parceling
of a dust mote in the eye and to cry
critical remarks assorted thirst
that had come about in a moment
addressed to himself alone

mix of this last by invention
formulates a transparency unfolds
regularly read in council
the recording of opinions

but that's how bob can already in plaster be guided along the garage
    way
layout of the offices everything was turned southward movements
    efforts
morning friction
packing tubes containing
a plaque develops the address of another location
time is up oxygen used up
his full length supported
he thought he saw across the walls
pictures
of earth and garden
lines them up
is not in flower
in the axis
and near the axis lines up
the eye
the length of a cable

straight radio of trajectories
estimated positions b as in bravo
summit add-on more lit up than he is
and not to be seen watch blow up

craving to remove the rings
and so do internal exercises

glass lenses
and proportionally large less
twelve
the ionic
air
easier
to use less
fussy

in the end he advised
easy does it the tight map
of thorax resin memo
stresses the rough-sketch

right now he has only one hair on his tongue
a permanent jingle bell
o how much
an intimidation attempt
neither attaches or chooses him

and that's how bob can with dazzling
see for himself that everything is unplugged
balloon hostess eternity effort
he can learn to stammer porpoise
there will be some p some p
some p some unknown pla
nets at the f at the f
at the f at the fol
low up of what the s the s
the s the s the sk
y is held together
with some ba some ba
some ba some ban
d-aids fallen
like confetti

aquarium carried off
simplification
no more need of the final kiss

            aquarium carried off
thick tube evacuation of rain water
the spirits who are there and by which ocean
                    in flower
the red city the delicious island
little paintbrush certain grain fibers
scales on brass rings on brass
                    in flower
the fish eats his meats
this greater strength for example
in his sight line
the floating organic look
                    in flower
the part cut off and by which ocean
the scarlet brain thrown out like a net

            aquarium carried off
he also has significant manufactured dreams signal mobilized
and against reason and against nature all the support
vertical suspension the ship creating a white path
he has silver hands and the knife that was carried for service
the super hot breath and directory assistance for thoughts

this effect when he affects
mailing
        in the manner
love often
whose eye takes in water

the day colors the programmatic sky
died of a grenade offensive

this effect when he affects
mailing
the ode about butterflies is once more cut off at the sea wall

mailing
wind assisting trailer
watch out you have lost your hankie

22

The test won't have slowed down the swerve
destination inside the house
does his best as a porter going all the way down
to the storeroom

the passing cable car
grows distant just overhead

disconnection of the index
at pyramid level
and the vast dome that was crushed
so the face in his proper name he ponders
the sky to the greater gods
that make things last this afternoon
the striking of a match
in this very dry place

the ray to melt the columns
does not reappear
makes him vocally lose
the coatroom job
it was a long time coming

but that's how bob can agitate the property titles
his "senior lumberjack" materials make use of the scenery
green coat in french
and resembles a body in mid-execution
stained door the luminous garden spreads comes back
the buying of mimosas mixes them up
condense
nobility
memoria approaching the point of safeguard
and dramatically he exits the train station
making exclamations

he could have corrected the poster mistakes
before the next world
all the eggs and jewels trailing
definitely consists of seeing the last act of the performance
before being sold off

repealing that's how he can deactivate the twitterings of birds
herald the inaugurated summer become beautiful girl ready for use
knows it the proof opening the eyes simplifies the whole spirit says
hey roughly makes the sound of cymbals leather podium repeated
    twice right there
what songs what songs rising in reverse his preference

first register cecil in the yellow cab
colorito silence o lyre she sings the friend with the eyedrops

second case filled with joy that makes the i in "rye" undeniable
not less enlightening that the role's awry in some undergrounds

no pedestal nor throne he opens the document configured of un-
    conscious behavior
with a word he appropriately closes the gap between the epistle to
    the corinthians and the soundproof booth

on the saint bartholomew site the story he records inserts the isolated
    parties
the tremolo effect on munich wood returns his story to its rough draft

to make a long story short someone touches his mug
the wheel the insults affect him like ax blows

it's a fact that the glad-handing of merchants could become the
    standard
small-fry diplomacy facing a bureau of interpretation

maximum force merchant ship special intermediary has no
place to attack rampart the brand breaks the frame another way

neutral elements the people the elbow grease takes him on relaxes him
secret suspense and technician and really keen he thinks

agent of his location
he makes a recording of one of his rooms
sedentary anatomy
where burns a fire
dog pose a sign of incubation

and that's how bob can moving house
finally really occupy himself with the lighting
whistle to the tune of "what ya think ya look like
                              on the meschacebe river . . . ."

gusts of wind
and grace tumbles

and then he tries
the name on the card

the frame of the card
the kind of ambiance

badges and fire-extinguishers
won't help here

the first matter
it it has disappeared

like life
only shorter

23

Necessary fragmentation of supplies
what he can say reused the firewall of which
the sample "escort service" is part
he has on the docks at the end of the harbor
demand no answer let's go
only one subject of conversation
and three shady characters for friends

not much is left of the perfection the panel
the angle he finds fascinating
in back the paint is not
what to put his mind to
should be kept built reconstituted in green wood

                    if the fetish
pulled from the "night kiss" chronicle
looks for pastures that match his ideas
is surprised by his insufficiencies the total number of jobs the
piracy
scrap metal will carry them away
admitted beforehand to parcel out the staging areas
to lean back on the wall
organ pipes of learned things

that's how he can in the final phase give proof of authority
force the ideal of decomposition on the same line all the time
light foot movement walking and with the docility
of a grand standing death he gives gifts conscious that he has
the little door a healthy air he remains delicate in the park
socks and with this distribution packet albert hall the finale
to represent himself he tacks on the glory-to-the-son machinery
                    visible plaque
            real augmentation of conditions
                  standard victory

the devotion that just got here
golden dragon on the bottom of the canal
gangsters's bullets
drowned rats

and that's how bob can think of something exciting
in the silence of the fourteenth floor
the modeling of careers
a metallic cable
big how
at which point
he chooses the first-aid option
hotel service
a brief pause during which
the habitual laws are recognized

a model of construction knocks on the opposite door
an anti-radiation suit
serves as a base for
the presentation of events
already arranged
really linked to the earth

the reception of diffusion disks
and what is made to disappear in the forest

and that's how he can on the plain
in inspecting the ground
study the terrestrial referential
confusion often
the same as accusing him

something more some
thing in the body's core totally
relaxes

something has gone through
the forest whistling
not the birds

definitely something living
from a past time the unfamiliar wing
of an airplane

to see clearly in detail that
fire still of winter
nine-

ty when we saw some
thing on the pond
good god

nothing of yore returns
before then its likely
we see

clearly something at last
and seen from the forest is the thing
that he took note of

considering the magnification the ultra-violet speed client
reincarnated
the light-colored body illusory is on his side
recuperates the peaceful elements in the dust

and he knows that the water has escalated
as high as the staircase
holds the body's suspension
remakes a complete character
the basement has several doors
the archeologist was radical enough
to go to bed with his house

answers time grace mania easily
mad stag
the costume of "captain universe"
makes the saved vase on the charger rock
answers the animals of creation
having given his name placed his paw
only way to establish
his paw truthfully what it is
exactly his paw
the attitude
of company
the encouragement of the negative
his expert gesture
in debt to the repetitions of the world
and relaxation

beautiful young trees straight in the eyes
and that's how bob can charming idea cordiality
stop in front of a portal

unabridged patagonian text
it's the distance from the honeyed resoling
overhang nothing to be seen no mark no trap
no sephora level with the pleura of a slaughter-bound roe-deer
ronsard merry christmas
tempo
moleskin
bird
you
us pollen

24

Right now he only has two basins filled with water
at three-quarters of an hour from two rivers
the remainder of the volume outside the sphere
he made a note of the place
of the air of the water
gigantic expansion
and the interruptions
far fewer now

right now he has
only two times two breaths
from time to time
on the fourth is heard
a peculiar two
time combination

localized partial punctual
less covered by a skull
on the earth having covered this earth
the rotating floor his head spinning
a middling walk-on part to master
which he labeled painful
to execute

that's how he can set up from a base to shoot in open country
across the distance reserved for shop windows
the embankment
it's a chance
and because of this
all the separate mutilations
that will reunite
quickly on a single face

the hour at which this operation took place
has dispersed him
in mirrors
without the initial of a new world

but that's how bob can with artificial respiration not see time pass
the mock-up is strong enough when daphne and the road goes there
represents the liaison that takes her on trips or won't budge for years
is not the authorized limit quitting which meant the past
when daphne was in the pleats of the same psyche he saw
the stuffed animal skeleton displaying its environment
and the footpath that leads here decided that that which was was

                       and he will have a sock-jaw sentiment
the harpsichord mechanism of a dead person when daphne had
started a second time and so with an empty cell
he starts turning for a long while episodically for all
pushing the merchandise to the cash register at the right moment
returns to the source his reserve a room or person
made him already late at night the correspondent in front of the door

                       and he will have a special dislocation
bring him where the growth on his temple alarms him
there was struggle and the doctor for some reason or other
didn't dare this reply delighted him when daphne
his opposite emblem made away by any means the theft of
yes but to have at his return other moments
this desire cuts him off as the way-too-involved delegate

and he will have a big dish-washer's bandana
which bothered this little nobody running
the face that daphne had thought his the penultimate
flight made that year a particular case
naturally covered with moss and conserved by thirds
made it scatter its erstwhile owner and cut down
will not have achieved one more time explores the montage

and he will have a shrinking scooter
from a big underground secret insisting on position to which point
and put in charge printing like a spy an exact specialized copy
the art of touching that he wants to come back to authorize diffusion
    there's no more
surface that would make a reflection his voice sounds similar more
    accurately recorded
and finally all devices like daphne made him
help himself to brains he was on the brink said it's coming

certain locations on display
to signal that he has recovered them
imitate a sound keep coming out
tracing the feudal smile in chalk

but that's how bob can gazelle accelerate in the final turnings
earth and scotland as mountain peak heroes
too close he is often also moral
freeze frame
a lovely leg tense with walking
three supplements and his satisfaction
sun's position he goes down

Biographical Notes:

Anne Portugal was born in Angers, in 1949. She lives and teaches in Paris where she is also recognized as one of the models in a famous "Poets' Calendar."

Her first collection, *La licence qu'on appelle autrement parrhésie,* appeared in the collective *Cahier de poésie* 3 (Gallimard, 1980). Since then Anne Portugal has published with P.O.L.:

Les commodités d'une banquette (1985)

De quoi faire un mur (1987)

Le plus simple appareil (1992)

Dans la reproduction en deux parties égales des plantes et des animaux (1999)

définitif bob, our present volume (2002).

In English:

Nude, trans. Norma Cole (Kelsey St. Press, 2001)

Quisite Moment, trans. Rosmarie Waldrop (Burning Deck, 2008)

Jennifer Moxley was born in San Diego and now lives and works in Maine. She is the author of the poetry collections, *Imagination Verse*s (Tender Buttons, 1996), *The Sense Record* (Edge, 2002), *Often Capital* (Flood Editions, 2005), *The Line* (Post-Apollo, 2007), and *Clampdown* (Flood Editions, 2009) as well as of a memoir, *The Middle Room* (Subpress, 2008).

She has translated Jacqueline Risset's book of poetry, *The Translation Begins* (Burning Deck, 1996) and her essays on sleep, *Sleep's Powers* (Ugly Duckling Press, 2008).